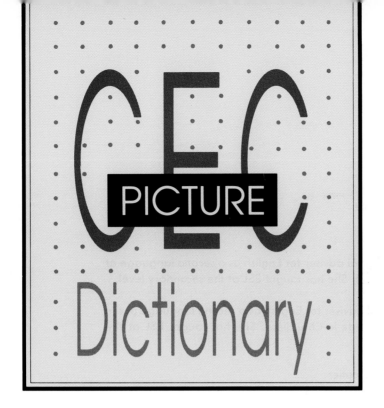

CEC PICTURE Dictionary

Hélène Blanchet
Suzanne Roy

Illustrated by

Pierre Brignaud
Ghislain Cloutier
Maurice Evans
Marguerite Gouin
François St-Germain
Studio de la Montagne

100 305 51

To Philippe and Brian
Benjamin, Pierre Luc and Maxime

Hélène Blanchet is a pedagogical adviser for English as a second language at the Commission scolaire Beauport. She has taught ESL at the secondary level.

Suzanne Roy is a pedagogical adviser for English as a second language at the Commission scolaire des Chutes-de-la-Chaudière. She has taught ESL at the primary and secondary levels.

Editors: Nancy Barr, Francine Cloutier

Design and art direction: Zapp

Illustrators: pp. 10, 15, 23, 62-63, 66: Pierre Brignaud; pp. 26-27, 58-59: Ghislain Cloutier; pp. 19, 36-39, 60: Maurice Evans; pp. 11-13, 22, 34, 35, 40-49, 52-53, 61: Marguerite Gouin; pp. 8-9, 20-21, 28-31, 50-51: Studio de la Montagne; pp. 6-7, 14, 16-19, 24-25, 32-33, 54-57, 64-65: François St-Germain.

©1990, by Centre Éducatif et Culturel inc.
8101, boul. Métropolitain est
Montréal (Québec) H1J 1J9

Dépôt légal: 2e trimestre 1990
Bibliothèque nationale du Québec
Bibliothèque nationale du Canada

ISBN 2-7617-0848-2

Printed in Canada

INTRODUCTION

The *CEC Picture Dictionary* illustrates over 800 carefully chosen words, all presented in lively, realistic situations. The book is designed for beginning learners of English as a second language. It is based on the idea that children learn new vocabulary best when words are presented in context rather than in isolation.

The *Dictionary* is organized around thirty-seven themes, with related topics grouped together. The topics include the world of play, school, home, animals, holidays and other subjects of interest to children.

Most themes feature a central picture that creates a scene. The Birthday Party, for example, shows a group of friends celebrating. Word labels are printed next to each lexical item selected: *birthday present, cake, balloon,* etc. In this way, the child does not have to ask for a native-language translation or search for the label elsewhere on the page.

The central picture is often accompanied by a series of illustrations in the margin that depict related vocabulary. In the case of The Birthday Party, useful verb phrases such as *make a wish* and *blow out the candle* are illustrated.

Some pages focus on categories rather than themes, for example, prepositions, adjectives, feelings and emotions, and question words. The *Dictionary* presents the items in context through illustrations and sentences or phrases that clarify meaning. To show *sad* in the unit Emotions and Feelings, a picture shows a boy looking unhappily at a flat tire with the caption *He is sad about his bike.*

The *CEC Picture Dictionary* is intended for students in the ESL class or for young learners at home. Parents, teachers and children can find out if a particular word is illustrated by referring to the indexes, one in English and one in French.

We hope that this book will help children build vocabularies and develop all English-language skills. The pictures and situations are designed to engage children in conversation, so we urge teachers and parents to use the *Dictionary* for discussion, word games and storytelling. Welcome to the delights of learning English!

Hélène Blanchet
Suzanne Roy

CONTENTS

THEME	TITLE	PAGE
Seasons and Weather	What's the weather like?	6-7
Clothing	Back-to-School Clothes	8-9
Getting Ready for School	Every Morning...	10
School	My New School	11
The Classroom	Our Class	12-13
School Supplies and Personal Identification	My School Bag	14
Numbers	Let's Count	15
Leisure-Time Activities	Hobbies and Pastimes	16-17
Halloween	Trick or Treat	18-19
The Human Body	From Head to Toe	20-21
Family	A Family Portrait	22
Emotions and Feelings	Ups and Downs	23
Birthdays and Colours	The Birthday Party	24-25
Occupations	When I Grow Up	26-27
The City	In and around the City	28-29
Winter Activities	Winter Carnival	30-31
Christmas, Hanukkah and Chinese New Year	Winter Celebrations	32-33
Hockey	After the Hockey Game	34
The Time and the Date	When is it? What time is it?	35
Outside the House	On the Weekend	36-37

THEME	TITLE	PAGE
Rooms of a House	**The House Next Door**	38-39
The Kitchen	**Grandma's Kitchen**	40
The Bedroom	**My Own Room**	41
Daily Activities	**Busy at Home**	42-43
Food and Drink	**Let's eat!**	44-45
Buying Vegetables	**The Vegetable Market**	46-47
Fruit and Desserts	**An Apple... or an Ice-Cream Cone?**	48-49
The Neighbourhood	**On My Street**	50-51
The Playground	**Let's Play**	52-53
Summer Vacation	**At the Lake**	54-55
Farm Animals	**The Petting Zoo**	56-57
Mammals	**Animals in the Wild**	58-59
Sea Animals, Reptiles and Birds	**Nature Study**	60
The Circus	**Fun at the Circus**	61
Prepositions	**Where are they?**	62-63
Descriptions	**Opposites**	64-65
Question Words	**Questions**	66
English Index		68
Index français		74

What's the weather like?

SPRING

storm clouds

lightning

forest

moose

fishing rod

It's raining.

worm

river

raindrop

fish

WINTER

It's snowing.

smoke

evergreen tree

snowflakes

ski

ski pole

mitten

tuque

icycle

snowman

shovel

SUMMER

sun

It's sunny.

island

CAMPSITE

tent

cooler

fire

firewood

picnic table

sleeping bag

bench

FALL/AUTUMN

It's windy.

sky

hunter

mountain

rifle

deer

Back-to-School Clothes

shirt

sweater

coat

pants

scarf

gloves

sock

boots

belt

store window

tie

a pair of shoes

BACK
TO
SCHOOL

SALE

blouse

dress

hat

jacket

skirt

raincoat

jeans

cap

glasses

T-shirt

shorts

running shoe

umbrella

shopping for clothes

9

Every Morning...

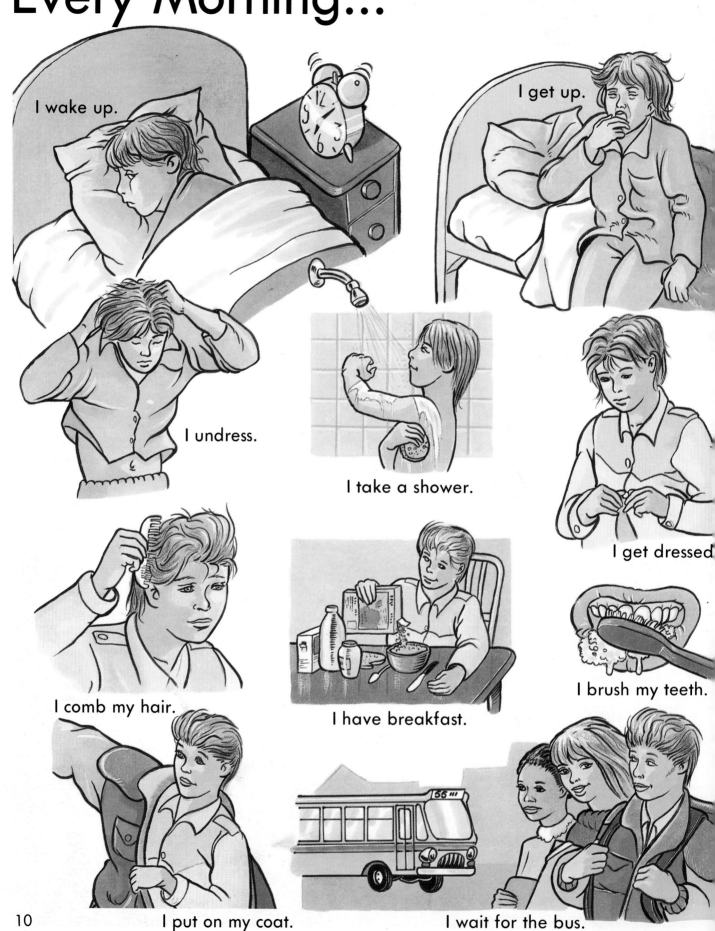

I wake up.

I get up.

I undress.

I take a shower.

I get dressed

I comb my hair.

I have breakfast.

I brush my teeth.

I put on my coat.

I wait for the bus.

10

My New School

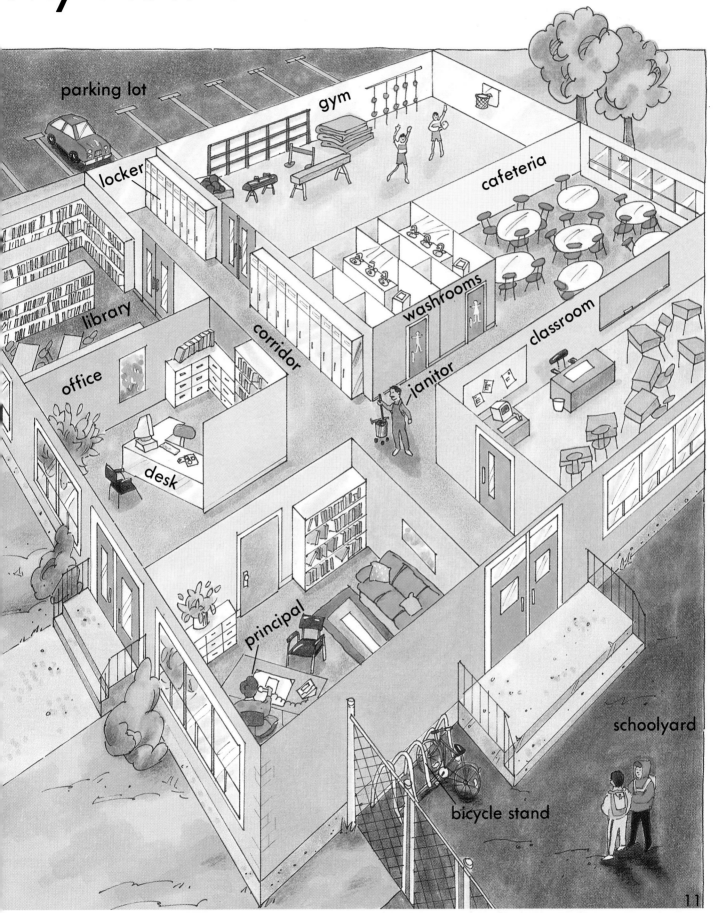

parking lot

gym

locker

cafeteria

library

corridor

washrooms

classroom

office

janitor

desk

principal

schoolyard

bicycle stand

11

Our Class

bulletin board

chalkboard

chalk

eraser

crayon

clock

teacher

erase

teach

draw

map

cassette player

desk

basket

cassett

talk

student

type

write

sleep

cut

colour

read

turn on/
turn off
the lights

bell

screen

shelf

pencil

computer

pencil sharpener

keyboard

paper

My School Bag

eraser

marker

cap

book

workbook

Maple St.

Name CHRISTINE CARPENTER
Grade 6
School WILFRED LA
Subject ENGLISH

label

11 YEARS OLD

Name: Chris Carpenter

Address: 689 Maple St.

Age: 11

Phone No: 555-4444

pencil

pen

ruler

ID card

555-4444

felt pen

notebook

paper clip

scissors

14

colouring pencils

Let's Count

one

two

three

four

five

six

seven

eight

nine

ten

eleven

twelve

thirteen

fourteen

fifteen

sixteen

seventeen

eighteen

nineteen

twenty

thirty

forty

fifty

sixty

seventy

eighty

ninety

one hundred

first

second

third

fourth

Hobbies and Pastimes

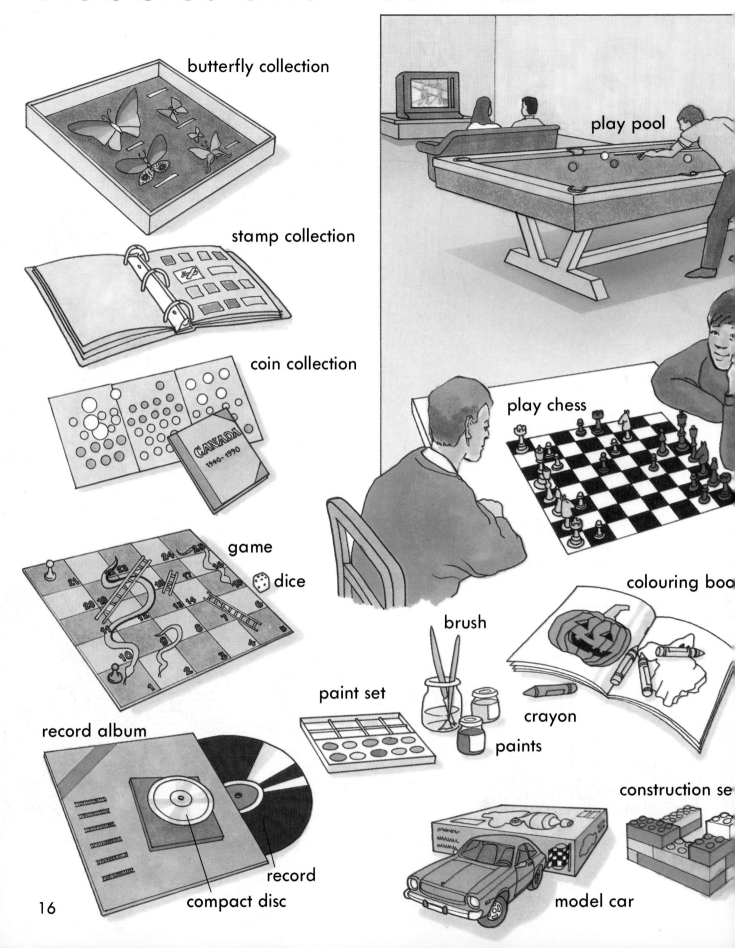

butterfly collection

stamp collection

coin collection

CANADA 1940 - 1990

game

dice

record album

record

compact disc

play pool

play chess

colouring boa

brush

paint set

crayon

paints

construction se

model car

16

ping-pong

paddle

play checkers

play cards

TV set

watch TV

magnifying glass

collect stamps

headphones

Walkman

listen to music

Trick or Treat

IN THE ATTIC

mice

beam

roller skates

witch

mask

bike

toys

chest

old clothes

airplane

trunk

ball

rocket

train set

19

From Head to Toe

cry

mouth

stomach

stand

pick up the bottle

Feeding the baby

nose

ear

should

arm

elbow

feet

foot

hair

chin

smile

cheek

tongue

lose a tooth

lip

babysitter

knee

walk

crawl

thumb

hand

finger

wave goodbye

or Dad!

mustache

beard

neck

ead

face

eye

climb

ouch your toes

heel

ankle

two teeth

eyebrow

bottom

hold a rattle

back

ody

leg

A Family Portrait

grandparents

grandmother

grandfather

aunt

father

parents

grandmother

grandfather

mother

uncle

children

cousin

sister

me

brother

Ups and Downs

How are you?

I'm **fine**, thanks.

He is **sick**.

Josh is **scared**.
He is **afraid** of the dog.

He is **angry**.

She is **shy**.

he is **embarrassed**.

You hurt me.

I'm **sorry**.

Mom is **happy**.

They are **tired**.

Surprise!

She is **surprised**.

He is **sad** about his bike.

23

The Birthday Party

hug

kiss

look up

birthday cake

make a wish

blow out
the candles

clap

spill

24

balloon

yellow

purple

green

brown

red

pink

orange

blue

black

Happy Birthday

e's thanking her friend.

birthday present

They're having fun.

sing

dance

laugh

When I Grow Up

singer

actor   actress

musician

construction worker

letter carrier

police officer

plumber

dentist

doctor

fire fighter

nurse

26 pilot

bus driver

taxicab driver

waiter   waitress

salesperson

farmer

fisherman

painter

butcher

baker

mechanic

electrician

hairdresser

photographer

scientist

secretary

garbage collector

dancer

reporter

computer programmer

In and around the City

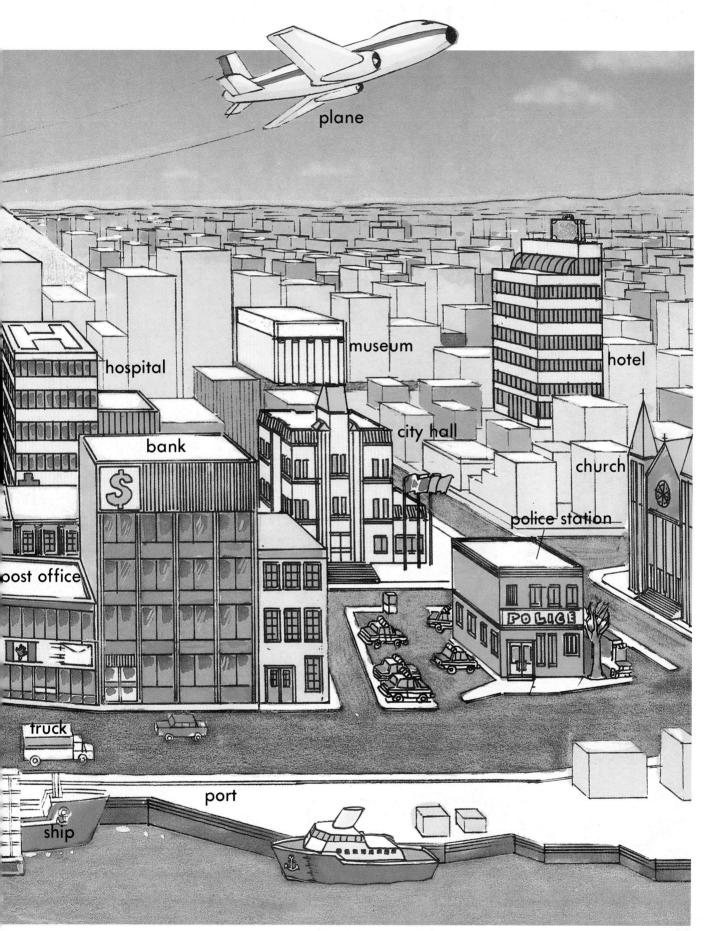

plane

hospital

museum

hotel

bank

city hall

church

police station

post office

POLICE

truck

port

ship

Winter Carnival

sledding

tobogganing

cross-country skiing

skating

snowblower

snowshoes

snow sculpture

king

queen

snowshoeing

making a snowman

sled

building an ice castle

toboggan

Winter Celebrations

star

CHRISTMAS

wreath

Christmas tree

ball

ornaments/
decorations

reindeer

bow

Santa Claus

sleigh

stocking

fireplace

lights

log

angel

manger

gifts/presents

ribbon

puppy

MERRY CHRISTMAS!

dragon

HANUKKAH

candle

menorah

card

HAPPY HANUKKAH!

lantern

CHINESE NEW YEAR

HAPPY NEW YEAR!

After the Hockey Game

coach

trainer

helmet

uniform

face mask

knee pads

shoulder pads

ice skate

hockey stick

puck

fall on the ice

skate

hockey player

net

goalie

score a goal

shoot

When is it? What time is it?

It's two o'clock.

When is your birthday?

JUNE

It's on Monday, June 20th.

A day

morning | afternoon | evening | night

What time is it?

It's seven-thirty by my watch.

On the Weekend

chimney

roof

lawn mower

mowing the lawn

window box

door

front yard

step

planting flowers

walking the dog

hedge

riding a bicycle

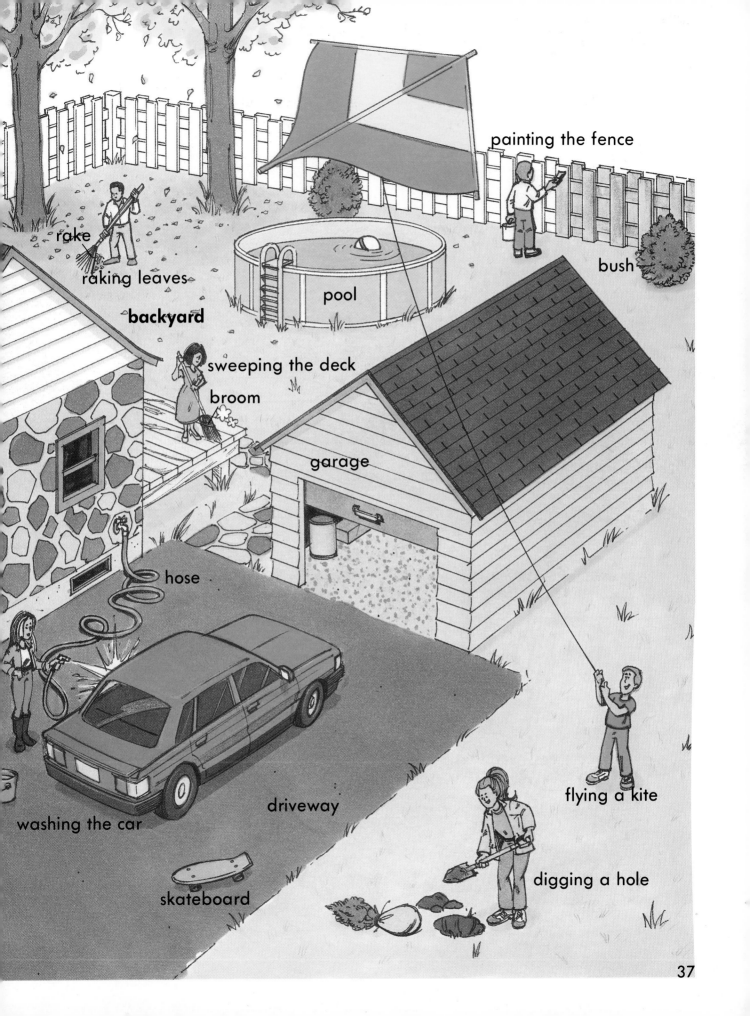

rake

raking leaves

backyard

painting the fence

bush

pool

sweeping the deck

broom

garage

hose

flying a kite

washing the car

driveway

skateboard

digging a hole

37

The House Next Door

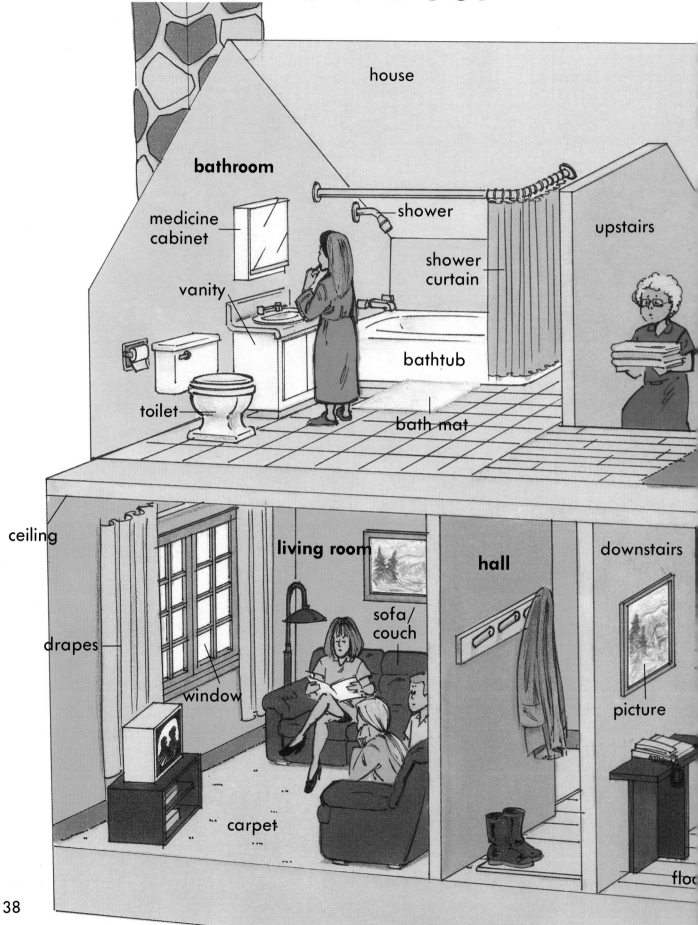

house

bathroom

medicine cabinet

shower

upstairs

vanity

shower curtain

bathtub

toilet

bath mat

ceiling

living room

hall

downstairs

drapes

sofa/couch

window

picture

carpet

floo

wall

bedroom

bed

telephone

night table

kitchen

stairs

dining room

table

stool

counter

chair

basement

39

Grandma's Kitchen

freezer

cookie jar

toaster

flowerpot

tap

sink

cupboard

handle

pan

radio

stove

knob

drawer

refrigerator

dishwasher

oven

teapot

tea

My Own Room

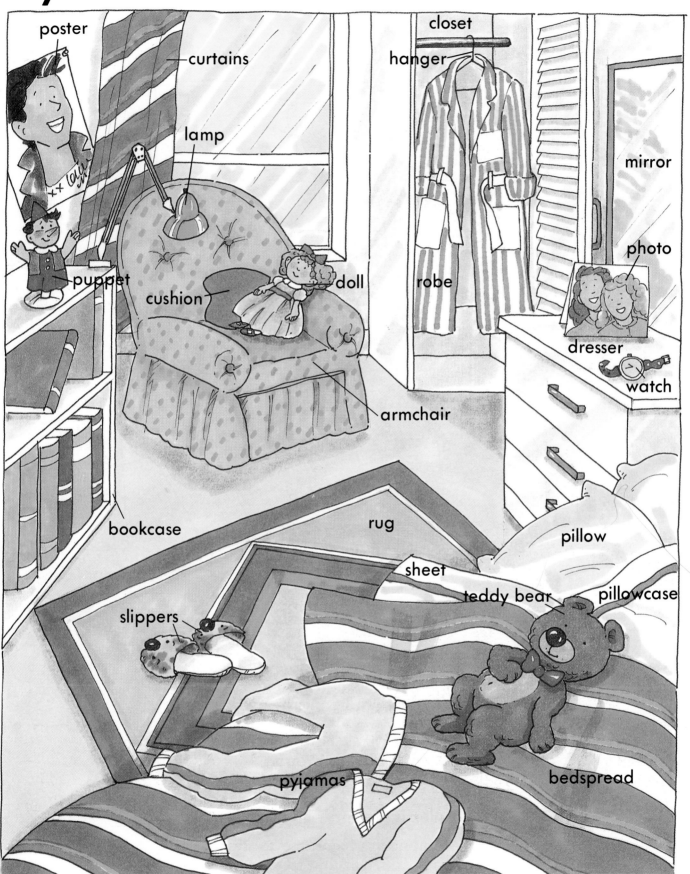

poster

curtains

lamp

closet

hanger

mirror

photo

robe

dresser

watch

puppet

cushion

doll

armchair

bookcase

rug

pillow

sheet

teddy bear

pillowcase

slippers

pyjamas

bedspread

Busy at Home

microwave oven

electric frying pan

wooden spoon

screwdriver

bucket

1 Leslie is frying eggs.
2 She's using the microwave.
3 Dad is stirring the soup.
4 Mom is baking bread.
5 Eric is cleaning up the mess.
6 Alex is playing with his toys.
7 Amanda is fixing the toaster.

oven mitts

4

washing the windows

setting the table

learning the alphabet

building a house

doing her homework

5

rag

taking care of the baby

Let's eat!

BREAKFAST

milk

butter

grapefruit

cereal

egg

toast

cheese

LUNCH

ham

bread

dish

loaf of bread

soft drink

straw

juice

SNACK

muffin

chocolate bar

raisins

yogurt

bowl

soup

SUPPER / DINNER

cup

fork

saucer

salad

rice

knife

fish

spoon

plate

placemat

45

The Vegetable Market

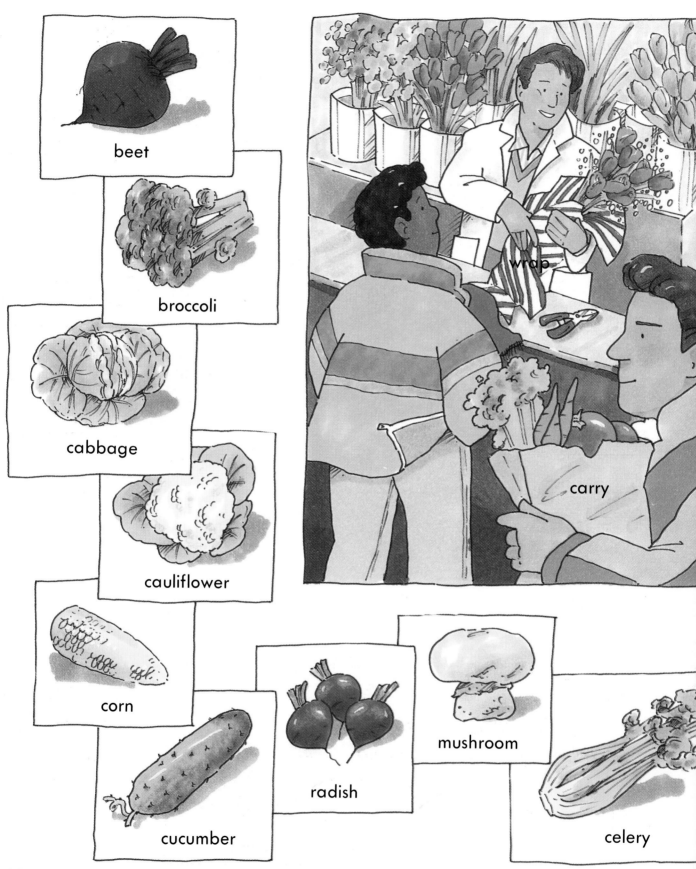

beet

broccoli

cabbage

cauliflower

corn

cucumber

radish

mushroom

celery

wrap

carry

buy

drop

lettuce

pumpkin

green beans

turnip

onion

peas

potato

tomato

carrot

An apple... or an ice-cream cone?

FRUIT

apple

plum

raspberry

lemon

banana

watermelon

pear

cherry

scale

cash register

orange

grapefruit

grapes

pineapple

strawberry

peach

blueberry

ASTRIES

cookie

doughnut

pie

cake

ICE CREAM

milkshake

sundae

chocolate sauce

cone

vanilla ice cream

On My Street

TO
RENT

street light

apartment

balcony

street sign

Park Ave.

Oak St.

sign

HATS BY LILY

store

parking meter

trash can

fire hydrant

mailbox

grass

staircase

street

50

building

tree

traffic light

bus stop

56
48
116

park

fence

stop sign

crosswalk

ticket

corner

sidewalk

garden

curb

51

Let's Play

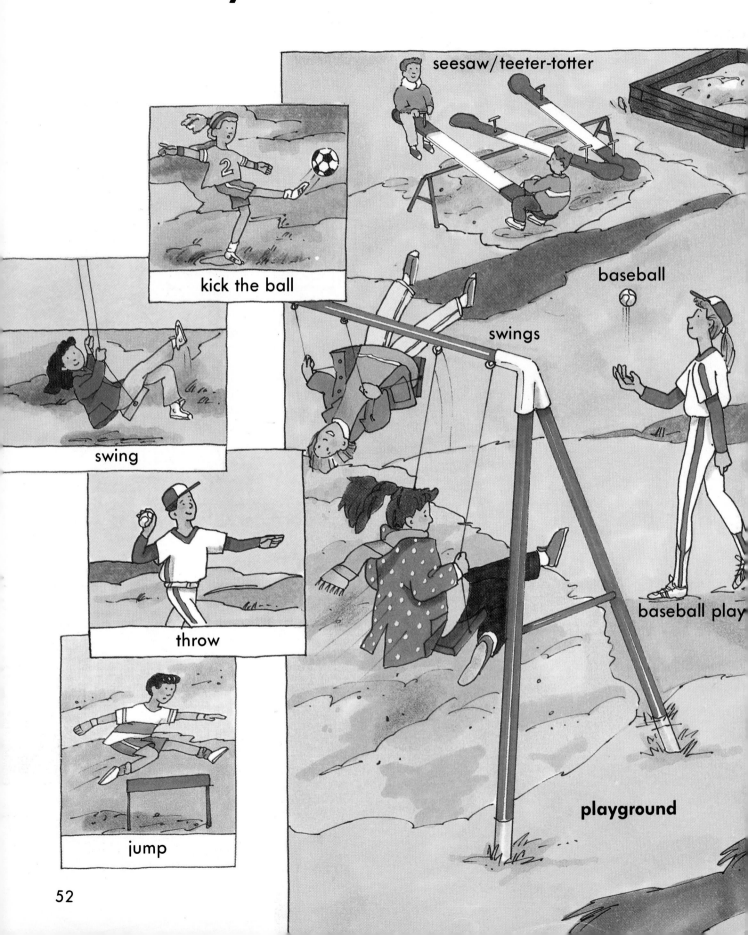

kick the ball

seesaw/teeter-totter

baseball

swings

swing

throw

baseball play

jump

playground

52

sandbox

soccer ball

glove

bat

slide

hit

catch

run

skip rope

53

At the Lake

cloud

woods

cottage

sail

lifeguard

rocks

life preserver

to play ball

to windsurf

oar

lake

beach

rowboat

sunburn

pail

sand

shovel

sunglasses

sandwic

beach towel

napkin

picnic basket

lifejacket

raft

ladder

to dive

sailboat

to sail

motorboat

to water-ski

to swim

bathing suit

having a picnic

blanket

The Petting Zoo

sheep

lamb

pig

tail

piglets

horse

colt

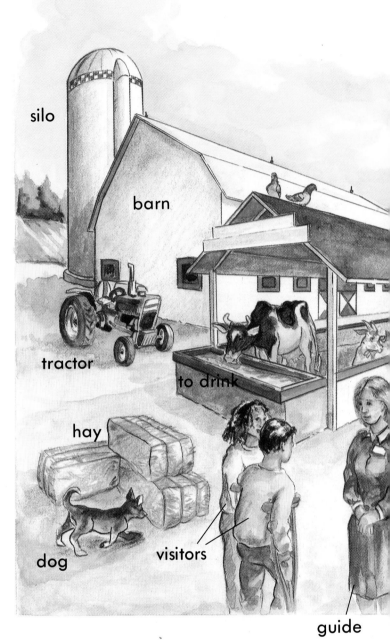

silo

barn

tractor

to drink

hay

dog

visitors

guide

cow

calf

horns

goat

kid

goose

wing

mane

pony

rabbit

paws

turkey

feathers

swallow

to fly

field

pond

stable

to brush

leash

to pet

goslings

duck

duckling

rooster

beak

chick

hen

57

Animals in the Wild

polar bear

camel

wolf

panda

hare

fox

hippopotamus

skunk

raccoon

gorilla

58

zebra

koala bear

tiger

beaver

monkey

deer

squirrel

giraffe

kangaroo

Nature Study

SEA ANIMALS

dolphin

seal

whale

crab

shark

lobster

starfish

turtle

lizard

frog

snake

REPTILES

BIRDS

seagull

owl

parrot

pigeon

penguin

Fun at the Circus

trapeze artist

ticket booth

trapeze

audience

monkey

cage

whip

elephant

lion

animal trainer

tiger

ball

seal

rabbit

clown

magician

Where are they?

above the clouds
over the clouds

between two girls

across the river

through the window...
into the soup

in the basket

out of the basket

behind the desk

beside the bar
next to the ba

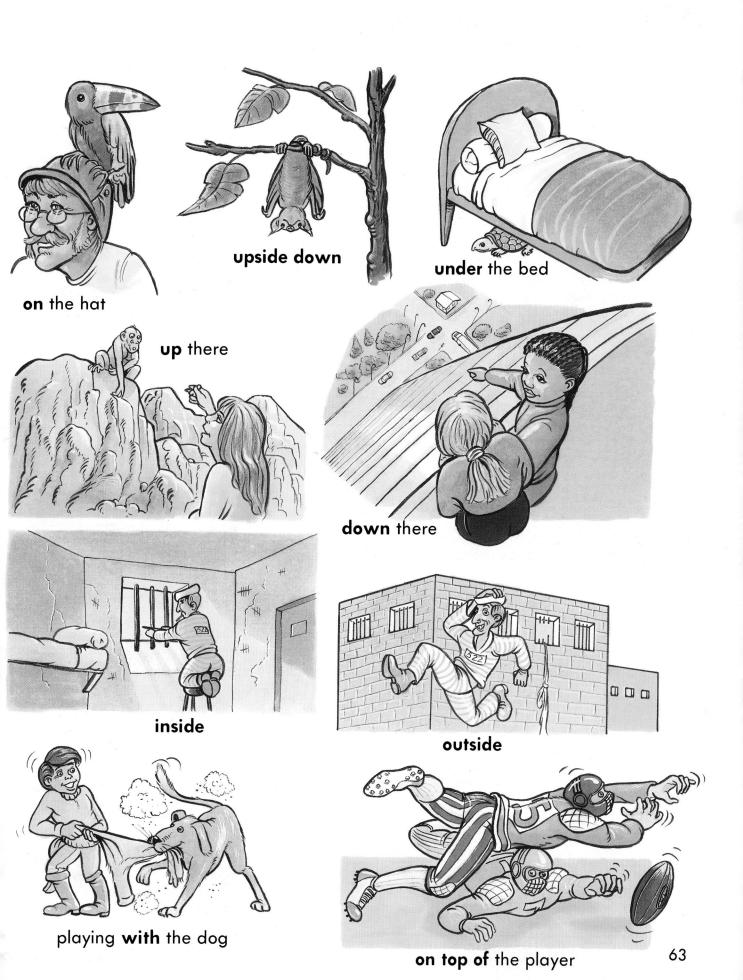

on the hat

upside down

under the bed

up there

down there

inside

outside

playing **with** the dog

on top of the player

63

Opposites

dirty   clean

short   long

old   new

curly   straight

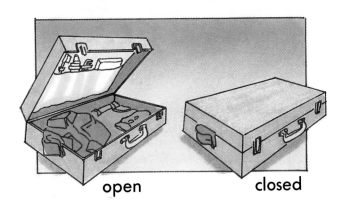

open   closed

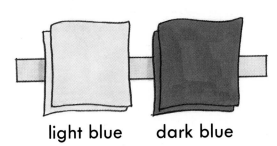

light blue   dark blue

64   beautiful   ugly

strong   weak

"This smells good."   "This smells bad."

hot   cold

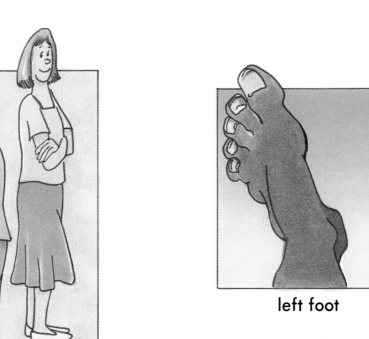

short   tall

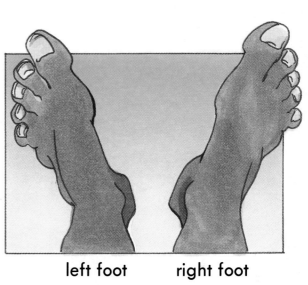

left foot   right foot

thin   fat

big   small/little   65

Questions

INDEXES

ENGLISH INDEX

This index lists in alphabetical order the words illustrated in the *CEC Picture Dictionary*. The number after each word refers to the page where the word is found.

Words that are illustrated in the plural, for example, *feathers*, are shown below with the plural form in parentheses: *feather(s)*. A word with more than one meaning is followed by an explanation in parentheses, for example, *swallow (bird)*. The abbreviations (*n.*) and (*v.*) refer to noun and verb.

A

above **62**
across **62**
actor **26**
actress **26**
address **14**
afraid **23**
afternoon **35**
age **14**
airplane **18**
airport **28**
alphabet **43**
angel **32**
angry **23**
animal **60**
animal trainer **61**
ankle **21**
apartment **50**
apple **48**
April **35**
arena **28**
arm **20**
armchair **41**
attic **18**
audience **61**
August **35**
aunt **22**
autumn **7**

B

baby **20, 43**
babysitter **20**
back (*n.*) **21**
backyard **37**

bad **65**
bake **42**
baker **27**
balcony **51**
ball **18, 52, 54, 61**
ball (Christmas) **32**
balloon **25**
banana **48**
bank **29**
barn **56**
baseball player **52**
basement **39**
basket (wastepaper) **12**
bat (animal) **19**
bat (baseball) **53**
bath mat **38**
bathing suit **55**
bathroom **38**
bathtub **38**
beach **54**
beach towel **54**
beak **57**
beam **18**
beard **21**
beautiful **64**
beaver **59**
bed **39**
bedroom **39**
bedspread **41**
beet **46**
behind **62**
bell **13**
belt **8**
bench **7**

beside **62**
between **62**
bicycle **36**
bicycle stand **11**
big **65**
bike **18**
bird **60**
birthday cake **24**
birthday present **25**
black **25**
blanket **55**
blouse **9**
blow out **24**
blue **25**
blueberry **48**
body **21**
book **14**
bookcase **41**
bookstore **28**
boots **8**
bottle (baby) **20**
bottom (*n.*) **21**
bow **32**
bowl **45**
bread **42, 44**
breakfast **44**
broccoli **46**
broom **37**
brother **22**
brown **25**
brush (*n.*) **16**
brush (*v.*) **57**
brush one's teeth **10**
bucket **42**

build **31, 43**
building **51**
bulletin board **12**
bus **28**
bus driver **26**
bus stop **51**
bush **37**
butcher **27**
butter **44**
butterfly **16**
buy **47**

C

cabbage **46**
cafeteria **11**
cage **61**
cake **49**
calf **56**
camel **58**
campsite **7**
candle **24, 33**
cap (clothes) **9**
cap (top) **14**
car **28, 37**
card (greeting) **33**
card(s) (playing) **17**
carpet **38**
carrot **47**
carry **46**
cash register **48**
cassette **12**
cassette player **12**
cat **19**
catch **53**

cauliflower **46**
ceiling **38**
celery **46**
cereal **44**
chair **39**
chalk **12**
chalkboard **12**
checkers **17**
cheek **20**
cheese **44**
cherry **48**
chess **16**
chest **18**
chick **57**
children (*sing.* child) **22**
chimney **36**
chin **20**
Chinese New Year **33**
chocolate bar **44**
chocolate sauce **49**
Christmas **32**
Christmas tree **32**
church **29**
circus **61**
city hall **29**
clap **24**
classroom **11**
clean (*adj.*) **64**
clean up **42**
climb **21**
clock **12**
closed **64**
closet **41**
clothes **18**
cloud **54**
clown **61**
coach **34**
coat **8, 10**
cobweb **19**
coin **16**
cold **65**
collect **17**
collection **16**
colour (*v.*) **13**
colouring book **16**
colouring pencil(s) **14**
colt **56**
comb (*v.*) **10**

compact disc **16**
computer **13**
computer program—
mer **27**
cone **49**
construction set **16**
construction worker **26**
cookie **49**
cookie jar **40**
cooler **7**
corn **46**
corner **51**
corridor **11**
costume **19**
cottage **54**
couch **38**
counter **39**
cousin **22**
cow **56**
crab **60**
crawl **21**
crayon **12, 16**
crib **19**
cross-country skiing **30**
crosswalk **51**
cry **20**
cucumber **46**
cup **45**
cupboard **40**
curb **51**
curly **64**
curtain(s) **41**
cushion **41**
cut (*v.*) **13**

D

Dad **21, 42**
dance **25**
dancer **27**
dark (*adj.*) **64**
day **35**
December **35**
deck **37**
decoration **32**
deer **7, 59**
dentist **26**
desk **11, 12**
dice **16**

dig a hole **37**
dining room **39**
dinner **45**
dirty **64**
dishse **44**
dishwasher **40**
dive **55**
do homework **43**
doctor **26**
dog **19, 36, 56**
doll **41**
dolphin **60**
door **36**
doughnut **49**
down **63**
downstairs **38**
dragon **32**
drapes **38**
draw **12**
drawer **40**
dress **9**
dress up **19**
dresser **41**
drink (*v.*) **56**
driveway **37**
drop **47**
drugstore **28**
duck **57**
duckling **57**

E

ear **20**
egg **42, 44**
eight **15**
eighteen **15**
eighty **15**
elbow **20**
electric frying pan **42**
electrician **27**
elephant **61**
eleven **15**
embarrassed **23**
erase **12**
eraser **12, 14**
evening **35**
evergreen tree **6**
eye **21**
eyebrow **21**

F

face **21**
face mask **34**
fall **34**
fall (season) **7**
farmer **27**
fat **65**
father **22**
feather(s) **57**
February **35**
feed **20**
feet **20**
felt pen **14**
fence **37, 51**
field **57**
fifteen **15**
fifty **15**
fine **23**
finger **21**
fire **7**
fire fighter **26**
fire hydrant **50**
fire station **28**
fireplace **32**
firewood **7**
first **15**
fish **6, 45**
fisherman **27**
fishing rod **6**
five **15**
fix **42**
floor **39**
flower(s) **36**
flowerpot **40**
fly (*v.*) **57**
fly a kite **37**
foot **20**
forest **6**
fork **45**
forty **15**
four **15**
fourteen **15**
fourth **15**
fox **58**
freezer **40**
Friday **35**
friend **25**
frog **60**

front yard   36
fruit   48
fry   42
fun   25

G

game   16
garage   37
garbage collector   27
garden   51
get dressed   10
get up   10
ghost   19
gift   32
giraffe   59
glasses   9
glove (baseball)   53
gloves   8
goal   34
goalie   34
goat   56
good   65
goose   56
gorilla   58
gosling   57
grade   14
grandfather   22
grandmother   22
grandparent(s)   22
grape(s)   48
grapefruit   44, 48
grass   50
green   25
green bean(s)   47
guide   56
gym   11

H

hair   20
hairdresser   27
hall   38
Halloween   19
ham   44
hand   21
handle   40
hanger   41
Hanukkah   33
happy   23

Happy birthday!   25
Happy Hanukkah!   33
Happy New Year!   33
hare   58
hat   9
have a picnic   55
have breakfast   10
have fun   25
hay   56
head   21
headphones   17
hedge   36
heel   21
helmet   34
hen   57
highway   28
hill   57
hippopotamus   58
hit   53
hockey player   34
hockey stick   34
hold   21
hole   37
homework   43
horn(s)   56
horse   56
hose   37
hospital   29
hot   65
hotel   29
house   38, 43
how many   66
how much   66
hug (v.)   24
hunter   7

I

ice   34
ice castle   31
ice cream   49
ice skate   34
icycle   6
ID card   14
in   62
inside   63
into   62
island   7

J

jack-o-lantern   19
jacket   9
janitor   11
January   35
jeans   9
juice   44
July   35
jump (v.)   52
June   35

K

kangaroo   59
keyboard   13
kick (v.)   52
kid (animal)   56
king   31
kiss (v.)   24
kitchen   39
kite   37
kitten   19
knee   21
knee pad(s)   34
knife   45
knob   40
koala bear   59

L

label   14
ladder   55
lake   54
lamb   56
lamp   41
lantern   33
laugh   25
lawn   36
lawn mower   36
leaves (sing. leaf)   37
learn   43
leash   57
left   65
leg   21
lemon   48
letter carrier   26
lettuce   47
library   11, 28
life preserver   54
lifeguard   54

litejacket   55
light (adj.)   64
light(s)   13, 32
lightning   6
lion   61
lip   20
listen   17
little   65
living room   38
lizard   60
loaf of bread   44
lobster   60
locker   11
log   32
long   64
look up   24
lose   20
lunch   44

M

magician   61
magnifying glass   17
mailbox   50
make a snowman   31
make a wish   24
mane   57
manger   32
map   12
March   35
marker   14
mask   18
mattress   19
May   35
me   22
mechanic   27
medicine cabinet   38
menorah   33
Merry Christmas!   32
mess (n.)   42
mice   18
microwave   42
microwave oven   42
milk   44
milkshake   49
mirror   41
mitten   6
model car   16
Mom   42

Monday **35**
monkey **59, 61**
monster **19**
month **35**
moose **6**
morning **35**
mother **22**
motorboat **55**
mountain **7**
mouse **18**
mouth **20**
movie theatre **28**
mow the lawn **36**
muffin **44**
museum **29**
mushroom **46**
music **17**
musician **26**
mustache **21**

N

name **14**
napkin **55**
neck **21**
net **34**
new **64**
next to **62**
night **35**
night table **39**
nine **15**
nineteen **15**
ninety **15**
nose **20**
notebook **14**
November **35**
nurse **26**

O

oar **55**
o'clock **35**
October **35**
office **11**
old **18, 64**
on **63**
on top of **63**
one **15**
one hundred **15**
onion **47**

open **64**
orange (colour) **25**
orange (fruit) **48**
ornament **32**
out of **62**
outside **63**
oven **40**
oven mitt **43**
over **62**
owl **60**

P

paddle **17**
pail **54**
paint set **16**
paint the fence **37**
paint(s) (*n.*) **16**
painter **27**
pair **8**
pan **40**
panda **58**
pants **8**
paper **13**
paper clip **14**
parent(s) **22**
park **51**
parking lot **11**
parking meter **50**
parrot **60**
pastries (*sing. pastry*) **49**
paw(s) **57**
pea(s) **47**
peach **48**
pear **48**
pen **14**
pencil **13, 14**
pencil sharpener **13**
penguin **60**
pet (*v.*) **57**
phone number **14**
photo **41**
photographer **27**
pick up **20**
picnic **55**
picnic basket **54**
picnic table **7**
picture **38**
pie **49**

pig **56**
pigeon **60**
piglet **56**
pillow **41**
pillowcase **41**
pilot **26**
pineapple **48**
ping-pong **17**
pink **25**
placemat **45**
plane **29**
plant flowers **36**
plate **45**
play **42**
play ball **54**
play cards **17**
play checkers **17**
play chess **16**
play pool **16**
playground **52**
plum **48**
plumber **26**
polar bear **58**
police officer **26**
police station **29**
pond **57**
pony **57**
pool (game) **17**
pool (swimming) **37**
poor **21**
port **29**
post office **29**
poster **41**
pot **40**
potato **47**
present (*n.*) **32**
principal **11**
puck **34**
pumpkin **47**
puppet **41**
puppy **32**
purple **25**
put on one's coat **10**
pyjamas **41**

Q

queen **31**

R

rabbit **57, 61**
raccoon **58**
radio **40**
radish **46**
raft **55**
rag **43**
raincoat **9**
raindrop **6**
rain (*v.*) **6**
raisin(s) **44**
rake (*n.*) **37**
rake leaves **37**
raspberry **48**
rattle **21**
read **13**
record **16**
record album **16**
red **25**
refrigerator **40**
reindeer **32**
reporter **27**
reptile **60**
restaurant **28**
ribbon **32**
rice **45**
ride a bicycle **36**
rifle **7**
right **65**
river **6**
robe **41**
rocket **18**
rock(s) **54**
roller skate(s) **18**
roof **36**
rooster **57**
row boat **54**
rug **41**
ruler **14**
run **53**
running shoe(s) **9**

S

sad **23**
sail (*n.*) **54**
sail (*v.*) **55**
sailboat **55**

salad   45
salesperson   27
sand   54
sandbox   53
sandwich   55
Santa Claus   32
Saturday   35
saucer   45
scale   48
scared   23
scarf   8, 19
school   14
schoolyard   11
scientist   27
scissors   14
score a goal   34
screen   13
screwdriver   42
sea animal   60
seagull   60
seal   60, 61
second   15
secretary   27
seesaw   52
September   35
set the table   43
seven   15
seventeen   15
seventy   15
shark   60
sheep   56
sheet   41
shelf   13
ship   29
shirt   8
shoot   34
shop (v.)   9
short   64, 65
shorts   9
shoulder   20
shoulder pad(s)   34
shovel   6, 54
shower   10, 38
shower curtain   38
shy   23
sick   23
sidewalk   51
sign   50

silo   56
sing   25
singer   26
sink   40
sister   22
six   15
sixteen   15
sixty   15
skate (v.)   34
skateboard   37
skating   30
skating rink   28
ski (n.)   6
ski pole   6
skip rope   53
skipping rope   19
skirt   9
skunk   58
sky   7
skyscraper   28
sled   31
sledding   30
sleep   13
sleeping bag   7
sleigh   32
slide (n.)   53
slipper(s)   41
small   65
smile   20
smoke   6
snack   44
snake   60
snow sculpture   30
snowblower   30
snowflake(s)   6
snow (v.)   6
snowman   6, 31
snowshoe(s)   30
snowshoeing   31
soccer ball   53
sock   8
sofa   38
soft drink   44
sorry   23
soup   42, 45
spider   19
spill   24
spoon   45

spring (season)   6
squirrel   59
stable   57
staircase   50
stairs   38
stamp   16
stand   20
star   32
starfish   60
straw   44
step (n.)   36
stir   42
stocking   32
stomach   20
stool   39
stop sign   51
store   50
store window   8
storm cloud(s)   6
stove   40
straight   64
strawberry   48
street   50
street light   50
street sign   50
strong   64
student   12
subject   14
summer   7
sun   7
sunburn   54
sundae   49
Sunday   35
sunglasses   54
sunny   7
supper   45
surprised   23
swallow (bird)   57
sweater   8
sweep the deck   37
swim   55
swing (v.)   52
swing(s) (n.)   52

T

T-shirt   9
table   39, 43
tail   56

take a shower   10
take care of   43
talk   13
tall   65
tap (n.)   40
taxicab driver   26
tea   40
teach   12
teacher   12
teapot   40
teddy bear   41
teeter-totter   52
teeth   10, 21
telephone   39
ten   15
tent   7
thank   25
thin   65
third   15
thirteen   15
thirty   15
three   15
through   62
throw   52
thumb   21
Thursday   35
ticket   51
ticket booth   61
tie (n.)   8
tiger   59, 61
time   35
tired   23
toast   44
toaster   40, 42
toboggan   31
tobogganing   30
toe   21
toilet   38
tomato   47
tongue   20
tooth   20
touch   21
toy(s)   18, 42
tractor   56
traffic light   51
train set   18
trainer   34
trapeze   61

72

trapeze artist **61**
trash can **50**
tree **51**
truck **29**
trunk **18**
Tuesday **35**
tuque **6**
turkey **57**
turn off the lights **13**
turn on the lights **13**
turnip **47**
turtle **60**
TV **17**
TV set **17**
twelve **15**
twenty **15**
two **15**
type (v.) **13**

U

ugly **64**
umbrella **9**
uncle **22**
under **63**
undress **10**
uniform **34**
up **63**
upside down **63**
upstairs **38**
use **42**

V

vanilla (ice cream) **49**
vanity **38**
visitor(s) **56**

W

wait for **10**
waiter **26**
waitress **26**
wake up **10**
walk **21**
walk the dog **36**
Walkman **17**
wall **38**
wash **37, 43**
washroom **11**
watch (n.) **41**

watch TV **17**
water-ski **55**
watermelon **48**
wave goodbye **21**
weak **64**
Wednesday **35**
week **35**
weekday **35**
weekend **35**
whale **60**
what **66**
when **35, 66**
where **66**
which **66**
whip **61**
who **66**
why **66**
window **38, 43**
window box **36**
windsurf **55**
windy **7**
wing **56**
winter **6**
wish (n.) **24**
witch **18**
with **63**
wolf **58**
wooden spoon **42**
woods **54**
workbook **14**
worm **6**
wrap **46**
wreath **32**
write **13**

Y

year **35**
year(s) old **14**
yellow **25**
yogurt **44**

Z

zebra **59**

INDEX FRANÇAIS

L'index des mots français permet de retrouver l'équivalent anglais par le numéro de page apparaissant à côté de chacun. Par exemple, si vous cherchez le mot anglais pour *fraise*, vous le trouverez illustré à la page 48 avec son équivalent *strawberry*.

Les formes féminines ou masculines différentes des noms et des adjectifs illustrés sont également données. Les formes féminines des noms désignant des emplois sont celles recommandées par l'Office de la langue française.

Les mots au pluriel dans les illustrations, par exemple *plumes*, apparaissent avec la forme plurielle entre parenthèses: *plume(s)*. Les mots ayant plus d'un sens sont suivis d'une explication entre parenthèses, par exemple, *bureau (meuble)*. Les abréviations *n.* et *v.* sont utilisées, au besoin, pour distinguer un nom d'un verbe.

A

acheter **47**
acteur **26**
actrice **26**
à côté de **62**
adresse **14**
aéroport **28**
affiche **41**
âge **14**
agneau **56**
agricultrice **27**
  agriculteur
aile **56**
à l'envers **63**
à l'extérieur **63**
à l'intérieur **63**
allumer la lumière **13**
alphabet **43**
amie **25**
  ami
ananas **48**
ange **32**
animaux marins **60**
  (animal marin)
année **14, 35**
an(s) **14**
août **35**
appartement **50**
applaudir **24**
apprendre **43**

après-midi **35**
araignée **19**
arbre **51**
arbre de Noël **32**
arbuste **36**
armoire **38, 40**
arrêt d'autobus **51**
assiette **45**
à travers **62**
attendre **10**
attraper **53**
au-dessus-de **62**
auto **28, 37**
autobus **10, 28**
automne **7**
autoroute **28**
avoir peur de **23**
avec **63**
avion **18, 29**
avril **35**

B

babillard **12**
baignoire **38**
baladeur **17**
balai **37**
balance **49**
balançoire(s) **52**
balançoire à bascule **52**
balayer la terrasse **37**

balcon **50**
baleine **60**
balle **18, 52**
ballon **25, 54, 61**
ballon de soccer **53**
banane **48**
banque **29**
barbe **21**
barre de chocolat **44**
bas de Noël **32**
bateau-moteur **55**
bâtir **31**
bâton de baseball **53**
bâton de hockey **34**
bâton de ski **6**
beau **64**
  belle
bébé **20, 43**
bec **57**
beignet **49**
betterave **46**
beurre **44**
biberon **20**
bibliothèque (pièce) **11**
bibliothèque (édifice) **28**
bibliothèque
  (meuble) **41**
bicyclette **18, 36**
bien **23**
billard **16**

biscuit **49**
bleu **25**
  bleue
bleuet **48**
blouse **9**
blouson **9**
boire **56**
bois **7**
boîte aux lettres **50**
boîte de couleurs **16**
bol **45**
bon **65**
bonhomme
  de neige **6, 31**
Bonne année! **33**
Bonne fête! **25**
bordure de trottoir **51**
borne-fontaine **50**
botte(s) **8**
bouche **20**
bouchère **27**
  boucher
boucle **32**
bouée de sauvetage **54**
bougie(s) **24**
boulanger-pâtissier **27**
  boulangère-pâtissière
boule de Noël **32**
boyau d'arrosage **37**
bras **20**

brocoli **46**
brosse à tableau **12**
brosser **57**
brun **25**
  brune
bûche **32**
bureau (meuble) **11**
bureau (pièce) **11**
bureau de poste **29**

C

cadeau d'anniversaire **25**
cadeau(x) **32**
cafétéria **11**
cage **61**
cahier **14**
cahier à colorier **16**
caisse **49**
camion **29**
canard **56**
caneton(s) **56**
canne à pêche **6**
capuchon **14**
caresser **57**
carotte **47**
carré de sable **53**
carte (souhait) **33**
carte d'identité **14**
carte géographique **12**
carte(s) (jeu) **17**
caserne de pompiers **28**
casier(s) **11**
casque **34**
casque d'écoute **17**
casquette **9**
cassette **12**
castor **59**
ceinture **8**
céleri **46**
cent **15**
centre sportif **28**
céréale(s) **44**
cerf-volant **37**
cerise **48**
chaise **39**
chalet **54**
chaloupe **54**

chambre **39**
chameau **58**
champ **57**
champignon **46**
chandail **8**
chandelle **33**
chanter **25**
chanteur **27**
  chanteuse
chapeau **9**
chasseur **7**
  chasseuse
chat **19**
château de glace **31**
chaton **19**
chaud **65**
  chaude
chaudière **42, 54**
chaudron **40**
chauffeur de taxi **26**
  chauffeuse de taxi
chauffeuse d'autobus **26**
  chauffeur d'autobus
chaussette **8**
chauve-souris **19**
cheminée **36**
chemise **8**
cheval **56**
cheveux **20**
cheville **21**
chèvre **56**
chevreau **56**
chevreuil **7, 59**
chien **19, 36, 56**
chiffon **43**
chiot **32**
chou (ruban) **32**
chou (légume) **46**
chou-fleur **46**
ciel **7**
cinéma **28**
cinq **15**
cinquante **15**
cintre **41**
ciseaux **14**
citron **48**
citrouille **47**
clavier **13**

clochette **13**
clôture **37, 51**
clown **61**
cochon **56**
cochonnet(s) **56**
coffre **18**
coiffeur **27**
  coiffeuse
coin de rue **51**
collation **44**
collection **16**
collectionner **17**
colline **57**
colorier **13**
combien **66**
commode **41**
compter un but **34**
comptoir **39**
concierge **11**
concombre **46**
congélateur **40**
construire **43**
contente **23**
  content
coq **57**
corbeille à papier **12**
corde à danser **19**
corne **56**
cornet **49**
corps **21**
corridor **11**
costume **19**
cou **21**
couchette **19**
coude **20**
couleuvre **60**
coup de soleil **54**
coupe glacée **49**
couper **13**
cour **37**
cour d'école **11**
courir **53**
couronne (Noël) **32**
court(s) **64**
  courte
cousin **22**
coussin **41**
couteau **45**

couvert **43**
couverture **54**
couvre-lit **41**
crabe **60**
craie **12**
cravate **8**
crayon **13, 14**
crayon(s) à colorier **14**
crayon de cire **12, 16**
crayon feutre **14**
crèche **32**
crème glacée **49**
crème glacée
  à la vanille **49**
creuser un trou **37**
crinière **57**
cuillère **45**
cuillère de bois **42**
cuisine **39**
cuisinière (objet) **40**

D

dactylographier **13**
dame(s) (jeu) **17**
dans **62**
danser **25**
danseuse **27**
  danseur
date **35**
dauphin **60**
dé **16**
décembre **35**
décoration(s) **32**
dégât **42**
déguiser **19**
déjeuner (n.) **44**
déjeuner (v.) **10**
de l'autre côté de **62**
dent(s) **10, 20, 21**
dentiste **26**
derrière **62**
dessiner **12**
deux **15**
deuxième **15**
devoir(s) **43**
dimanche **35**
dinde **57**
dîner **44**

directrice **11**
  directeur
disque **16**
disque compact **16**
divan **38**
dix **15**
dix-huit **15**
dix-neuf **15**
dix-sept **15**
doigt **21**
dompteur **61**
  dompteuse
donner un
  coup de pied **52**
dormir **13**
dos **21**
douche **10, 38**
douze **15**
dragon **32**
drap **41**
droit **65**
  droite

E

eau gazeuse **44**
éboueur **27**
  éboueuse
échapper **47**
échecs (jeu) **16**
échelle **55**
éclair **6**
école **14**
écouter
  de la musique **17**
écran **13**
écrire **13**
écureuil **59**
écurie **57**
effacer **12**
église **29**
électricien **27**
  électricienne
éléphant **61**
élève **13**
emballer **46**
embrasser **25**
en bas **38, 63**
en dehors de **62**

enfant(s) **22**
en haut **38, 63**
enseignante **12**
  enseignant
enseigne **50**
enseigner **12**
entraîneur **34**
  entraîneuse
entre **62**
entrée (voiture) **37**
entrée (maison) **38**
envoyer la main **21**
épaule **20**
épaulière(s) **34**
épi de maïs **46**
escalier **39, 50**
espadrille(s) **9**
étable **56**
étagère **13**
étang **57**
été **6**
éteindre la lumière **13**
étiquette **14**
étoile **32**
étoile de mer **60**
évier **40**

F

fâché **23**
  fâchée
facteur **26**
  factrice
faible **64**
faire cuire **42**
faire de la bicyclette **36**
faire de la planche à
  voile **55**
faire de la raquette **31**
faire de la voile **55**
faire du ski de fond **30**
faire du ski nautique **55**
faire frire **42**
faire ses devoirs **43**
faire soleil **7**
faire un bonhomme
  de neige **31**
faire un pique-nique **55**
faire un souhait **24**

faire voler
  un cerf-volant **37**
fantôme **19**
fatiguée(s) **23**
  fatigué
fauteuil **41**
fenêtre **38, 43**
fermée **64**
  fermé
fesse(s) **21**
feu de camp **7**
feu de circulation **51**
feuille(s) **37**
février **35**
filet **34**
fin de semaine **35**
fleur(s) **36**
flocon(s) de neige **6**
foin **56**
foncé **64**
forêt **6, 54**
fort **64**
  forte
fouet **61**
foulard **8, 18**
four **40**
four micro-ondes **42**
fourchette **45**
foyer **32**
fraise **48**
framboise **48**
frapper **53**
frère **22**
frisé(s) **64**
  frisée
froid **65**
  froide
fromage **44**
fruit(s) **48**
fumée **6**
fusée **18**
fusil **7**

G

gant (baseball) **53**
gant(s) **8**
garage **37**
garde-robe **41**

gardien de but **34**
  gardienne de but
gardienne **20**
  gardien
gâteau **49**
gâteau d'anniversaire **24**
gauche **65**
gazon **36**
gênée **23**
  gêné
genou **21**
genouillière **34**
gilet de sauvetage **55**
girafe **59**
glace **34**
glacière **7**
glaçon **6**
glisser en traîne **30**
glisser en traîneau **30**
glissoire **53**
goéland **60**
gomme à effacer **14**
gorille **58**
goutte de pluie **6**
grande **64**
  grand
grand-mère **22**
grand-père **22**
grands-parents **22**
gras **64**
  grasse
gratte-ciel **28**
grenier **18**
grenouille **60**
grille-pain **40, 42**
grimper **21**
gros **65**
  grosse
guichet **61**
guide **56**
gymnase **11**

H

haie **36**
Halloween **19**
Hanoukka **33**
haricot(s) vert(s) **47**
heure(s) **35**

hibou **60**
hippopotame **58**
hirondelle **57**
hiver **6**
hochet **21**
homard **60**
hôpital **28**
horloge **12**
hôtel **29**
hôtel de ville **29**
huit **15**

I

île **7**
immeuble **51**
imperméable **9**
infirmière **26**
  infirmier

J

jambe **21**
jambon **44**
janvier **35**
jardin **51**
jardinière (objet) **36**
jarre à biscuits **40**
jaune **25**
jean(s) **9**
jeu **16**
jeu de construction **16**
jeudi **35**
joue **20**
jouer **42**
jouer au ballon **54**
jouer au billard **16**
jouer aux cartes **17**
jouer aux dames **17**
jouer aux échecs **16**
jouet(s) **18, 42**
joueur de hockey **34**
  joueuse de hockey
joueuse de baseball **52**
  joueur de baseball
jour **35**
jour de l'An chinois **33**
journaliste **27**
journée **35**
Joyeuse Hanoukka! **33**

Joyeux Noël! **32**
juillet **35**
juin **35**
jupe **9**
jus **44**

K

kangourou **59**
koala **59**

L

lac **54**
laid **64**
  laide
laisse **57**
lait **44**
lait fouetté **49**
laitue **47**
lampadaire **51**
lampe **41**
lancer (rondelle) **34**
lancer (balle) **52**
langue **20**
lanterne (Halloween) **19**
lanterne vénitienne **33**
lapin **57, 61**
lave-vaisselle **40**
laver **37, 43**
lèvre(s) **20**
lézard **60**
librairie **28**
lièvre **58**
lion **61**
lire **13**
lit **39**
livre **14**
long(s) **64**
  longue
loup **58**
loupe **17**
lumière **13, 32**
lundi **35**
lunettes **9**

M

magasin **50**
magasiner
magicien **61**

magnétophone **12**
mai **35**
maillot de bain **55**
main **21**
maison **38, 43**
maître-nageur **54**
  maître-nageuse
malade **23**
malle **18**
maman **42**
manteau **8, 10**
marcher **21**
mardi **35**
marionnette **41**
marqueur **14**
mars **35**
masque
  (déguisement) **18**
masque (protection) **34**
matelas **19**
matière **14**
matin **35**
mauvais **65**
mécanicienne **27**
  mécanicien
médecin **26**
melon d'eau **48**
menora **33**
menton **20**
mercredi **35**
mère **22**
mettre en marche **42**
mettre le couvert **43**
mettre son manteau **10**
mince **64**
miroir **41**
mitaine **6**
mitaine pour le four **43**
modèle réduit **16**
moi **22**
mois **35**
monnaie(s) **16**
monstre **19**
montagne **7**
montre **41**
moufette **58**
moustache **21**
mouton **56**

muffin **44**
mur **38**
musée **29**
musicienne **26**
  musicien

N

nager **55**
napperon **45**
navet **47**
navire **29**
neiger **6**
nettoyer **42**
neuf (nombre) **15**
neuve **64**
  neuf
nez **20**
Noël **32**
noir **25**
  noire
nom **14**
nourrir **20**
novembre **35**
nuage **54**
nuit **35**
numéro de téléphone **14**

O

octobre **35**
oeil **21**
oeuf(s) **42, 44**
oie **56**
oignon **47**
oiseau(x) **60**
oison(s) **57**
oncle **22**
onze **15**
orangé **25**
  orangée
orange **48**
ordinateur **13**
oreille **20**
oreiller **41**
orignal **6**
orteil(s) **21**
où **66**
ours polaire **58**

ourson **41**
ouverte **64**
  ouvert
ouvrier de la
  construction **26**
  ouvrière

P

paille **44**
pain **42, 44**
paire **8**
pâle **64**
pamplemousse **44, 48**
panda **58**
panier à pique-nique **54**
panneau d'arrêt **51**
pantalon **8**
pantoufle(s) **41**
papa **21, 42**
papier **13**
papillon(s) **16**
par-dessus **63**
parapluie **9**
parc **51**
parcomètre **51**
parents **22**
parler **13**
passage
  pour piétons **51**
patin **34**
patin(s) à roulettes **18**
patiner **31, 34**
patinoire **28**
pâtisserie(s) **48**
patte(s) **57**
pauvre **21**
pêche **48**
pêcheur **27**
  pêcheuse
peindre la clôture **37**
peintre en bâtiment **27**
pelle **6, 54**
pelouse **50**
perdre **20**
père **22**
Père Noël **32**
perroquet **60**

petit **65**
  petite
peur **23**
pharmacie (magasin) **28**
pharmacie (armoire) **38**
phoque **60, 61**
photo **41**
photographe **27**
pied **20**
pigeon **60**
pilote **26**
pinceau **16**
pingouin **60**
ping-pong **17**
pique-nique **55**
piscine **37**
plafond **38**
plage **54**
planche à voile **55**
plancher **38**
planter des fleurs **36**
plaque de rue **50**
pleurer **20**
pleuvoir **6**
plombier **26**
  plombière
plonger **55**
plume(s) **57**
pochette (disque) **16**
poêle à frire **40**
poêle à frire
  électrique **42**
poignée (chaudron) **40**
poignée (tiroir) **40**
poire **48**
pois **47**
poisson **6, 45**
policière **26**
  policier
pomme **48**
pomme de terre **47**
pompier **26**
  pompière
poney **57**
port **29**
porte **36**
porter **46**
poste de police **29**

pot de fleurs **40**
pot(s) de peinture **16**
poubelle **50**
pouce **21**
poulain **56**
poule **57**
poupée **41**
pourquoi **66**
poussin **57**
poutre **18**
premier **15**
  première
prendre soin de **43**
prendre une douche **10**
printemps **6**
programmeur **27**
  programmeuse
promener le chien **36**
propre(s) **64**
prune **48**
public **61**
pupitre **12**
pyjama **41**

Q

quand **66**
quarante **15**
quatorze **15**
quatre **15**
quatre-vingt-dix **15**
quatre-vingts **15**
quatrième **15**
quel **66**
quelle **35, 66**
qu'est-ce-que **66**
queue **56**
qui **66**
quinze **15**

R

radeau **55**
radio **40**
radis **46**
raide(s) **64**
raisin(s) **48**
raisin(s) sec(s) **44**
ramasser **20**
rame **54**

ramper **21**
raquette
  (ping-pong) **17**
raquette(s)
  (sport d'hiver) **30, 31**
râteau **37**
râteler les feuilles **37**
raton laveur **58**
réfrigérateur **40**
regarder **24**
regarder la
  télévision **17**
règle **14**
reine **31**
remercier **25**
remuer **42**
renard **58**
renne **32**
renverser **24**
réparer **42**
reptile(s) **60**
requin **60**
restaurant **28**
rideau de douche **38**
rideau(x) **41**
rire **25**
rivière **6**
riz **45**
robe **9**
robe de chambre **41**
robinet **40**
rocher(s) **54**
roi **31**
rondelle **34**
rose **25**
rôtie **44**
rouge **25**
rouli-roulant **37**
ruban **32**
rue **51**

S

sable **54**
sac de couchage **7**
s'amuser **25**
salade **45**
sale(s) **64**
salle à manger **39**

salle de bain **38**
salle de classe **11**
salon **38**
samedi **35**
sandwich **54**
sapin **6**
sauce au chocolat **49**
sauter **52**
sauter à la corde **53**
scientifique **27**
sculpture de neige **30**
seau **42, 54**
se balancer **52**
se brosser les dents **10**
secrétaire **27**
se déshabiller **10**
seize **15**
se lever **10**
semaine **35**
se peigner **10**
sept **15**
septembre **35**
serrer dans ses bras **24**
se réveiller **10**
serveur **26**
serveuse **26**
serviette de plage **54**
serviette de table **54**
se tenir debout **20**
seuil **36**
s'habiller **10**
short **9**
silo **56**
singe **59, 61**
six **15**
ski **6**
ski de fond **30**
ski nautique **55**
soeur **22**
soigneur **34**
 soigneuse
soir **35**
soixante **15**
soixante-dix **15**
soleil **7**
sorcière **18**
soucoupe **45**
souffler **24**

souffleuse **30**
souhait **24**
soulier(s) **8**
soupe **42, 45**
souper (n.) **45**
sourcil **21**
sourire **20**
souris **18**
sous **63**
sous-sol **39**
stationnement **11**
stylo **14**
support pour
 bicyclettes **11**
sur **63**
surprise **23**
 surpris

T

table **39**
table de chevet **38**
tableau (noir) **13**
tableau (art) **38**
tabouret **39**
taie d'oreiller **41**
taille-crayons **13**
talon **21**
tante **22**
tapis **38, 41**
tapis de bain **38**
tarte **49**
tasse **45**
téléphone **39**
téléviseur **17**
tenir **21**
tente **7**
tenture(s) **38**
terrain de camping **7**
terrain de jeu **52**
terrasse **37**
tête **21**
thé **40**
théière **40**
tigre **59, 61**
timbre(s) **16, 17**
timide **23**
tiroir **40**
toile d'araignée **19**

toilette (objet) **38**
toilette(s) (pièce) **11**
toit **36**
tomate **47**
tomber **34**
tondeuse **37**
tondre le gazon **36**
tortue **60**
toucher **21**
tournevis **42**
tracteur **56**
train **18**
traîne **31**
traîneau **31, 32**
trapèze **61**
trapéziste **61**
treize **15**
trente **15**
triste **23**
trois **15**
troisième **15**
trombone **14**
trottoir **51**
trou **37**
t-shirt **9**
tuque **6**

U

un **15**
uniforme **34**

V

vache **56**
vaisselle **44**
veau **56**
vendeur **27**
 vendeuse
vendredi **35**
venter **7**
ventre **20**
ver **6**
verres fumés **54**
vert **25**
 verte
vêtement(s) **18**
vieille **64**
vieux **18**
vingt **15**

violet **25**
visage **21**
visiteur(s) **56**
vitrine **8**
voile **54, 55**
voilier **55**
voler **57**

Y

yeux **21**
yogourt **44**

Z

zèbre **59**